Think Before You Stink

By
Tahrita Barron

Printed in the United States of America.

First Printing, December 2020

ISBN: 978-1-7358024-6-6

Author: Tahrita Barron

Editer: Katherine A. Young

Illustrator: Hatice Bayramoglu

Assisted by: Write It Out Publishing LLC

Tahritabarron.com

Dedication

I would like to dedicate this book to all children who may have felt lonely, distant, abandoned, neglected, abused, and misunderstood. I want the children who have experience loss, hurt, pain, and sorrow to know that they are loved no matter where they go, no matter how far they may stay away from home, no matter what they do someone cares for them, and his name is Jesus. I want the children who have never heard or felt the love of Jesus to experience and feel it when they or when someone reads this book to them. Children are a gift from God and they have a purpose and calling on each and every one of their lives. In addition, there are children who have military moms and dads and have to face the challenges of being separated from each for periods of time and this is an opportunity to reach your child or someone's child they know by putting a smile on their face and warmth in their heart.

To my husband: I would like to thank you for your sweat, tears, and prayers that caused you to persevere and support my dreams. I love you.

To my children: Arilla, Freddy Jr., Daniel, Fiona, Jasmine, and Janessa, your mommy loves you dearly and I pray for nothing but the best for you. We have come a long way.

Yesterday on a Sunday afternoon, I got so upset at my baby brother.

My mom told me to clean my room, but she doesn't realize that when my baby brother comes in the room to play, he makes a BIG MESS.

That is exactly what happened. I cleaned up my room and my baby brother made a BIG MESS!

SLAM!
I got so mad that I slammed the door so hard that the entire house would feel how angry I was.
Only problem, well, multiple problems with me slamming the door so hard that the entire house would feel what I felt was that I made my baby brother cry! Oh no!

Not only did I stink, but I noticed that when I went to take a shower, I still stunk!

When I went to put deodorant on, I still stunk!

When I went to brush my teeth, I still stunk!

When I sprayed on some perfume, I still stunk!

When I went to bed, I still stunk.

When I woke up the next morning to get ready for school, I still stunk! This can't be!

There is no way I can go to school smelling like this! While I was panicking, I could hear my baby brother in the next room in his crib babbling and making baby sounds as he began to wake up.

The baby brother looked up at me and said with his eyes, *It's okay. I forgive you—just always remember to think before you stink.*

Immediately the horrible smell went away, and I didn't stink anymore!

So, the next time before you make a decision, think about what could happen and remember to think before you stink!

What can you do to think before you Stink?

www.ingramcontent.com/pod-product-compliance
Lightning Source LLC
Chambersburg PA
CBHW060800150426
42813CB00058B/2773

* 9 7 8 1 7 3 5 8 0 2 4 6 6 *